# Coping *with* Chaos *workbook*

## Facilitator Reproducible Guided Self-Exploration Activities

Ester R.A. Leutenberg
& John J. Liptak, EdD

Illustrated by Amy L. Brodsky, LISW-S

**Whole Person Associates**

101 West 2nd Street, Ste 203
Duluth, MN 55802

800-247-6789

Books@WholePerson.com
WholePerson.com

**Coping with Chaos Workbook**
Facilitator Reproducible Guided Self-Exploration Activities

Copyright ©2013 by Ester R.A. Leutenberg and John J. Liptak. All rights reserved. Except for short excerpts for review purposes and materials in the assessment, journaling activities, and educational handouts sections, no part of this book may be reproduced or transmitted in any form by any means, electronic or mechanical without permission in writing from the publisher. Self-assessments, exercises, and educational handouts are meant to be photocopied.

All efforts have been made to ensure accuracy of the information contained in this book as of the date published. The author(s) and the publisher expressly disclaim responsibility for any adverse effects arising from the use or application of the information contained herein.

Printed in the United States of America

Editorial Director: Carlene Sippola
Art Director: Joy Morgan Dey

Library of Congress Control Number: 2013936469
ISBN: 978-157025-298-3

# Coping with Chaos Introduction

# Using This Book

> DEFINITION OF CHAOS: a state of utter confusion; complete disorder; a jumble.

One thing that all people can count on in the twenty-first century is living with chaos. Chaos refers to a state of confusion in your life, the experience of random or unpredictable occurances, and/or a lack of order to your daily life, space and belongings. Chaos can be seen in the many changes in the workplace, cell phones ringing and people constantly beset with interruptions, the barrage of new information flooding into your brain, thousands of choices, new and improved product ideas, new technologies that arrive daily, and new family structures. Often a family member volunteers or is forced to take on a new role such as caregiving. These are just a few of the many ways people are experiencing increased chaos in their lives which leaves them feeling irritated, frustrated, exhausted, angry, overwhelmed and/or confused.

Many people are interested in returning to the days when life was simpler, calmer, more controllable and more predictable. People want their lives to be full of events, people, and things they can predict and count on. Instead, they feel like they are losing their sense of purpose, control and predictability, and the result of these feelings is a sense of exasperation and weariness.

Faced with many choices, loads of information at everyone's fingertips, and complex technological systems, people seek to establish order and control in their chaotic lives. More than ever before, it is important to understand chaos and attempt to find patterns in the chaos.

**This can be seen throughout history:**

- **Religion** – Various religions have tried to make sense of the world by coming to terms with evil and making sense of a world that seems aimless, violent, and full of random acts and events.

- **Science** – The history of science is an ongoing attempt to discover patterns in the physical world and to understand incomprehensible and disorderly events. Scientists usually spend their lives searching for laws and patterns that can be repeated and therefore understood.

- **Mythology** – Myths have been handed down through the ages to help cultures make sense of the randomness of events. Myths include parables related to birth, death, journeys to distant lands, magical beasts, mythical heroes and heroines, and gods and goddesses.

People often ask, "Why worry about chaos, there's nothing you can do about it?" The fact is that people can control the chaos in their lives. It can be quite liberating to realize that chaos, although unsettling, need not be as frustrating as people believe they can learn to define patterns of chaos and redirect their energies and abilities.

# Coping with Chaos Introduction

## A New Way of Looking at Chaos

The Chaos Theory is one of the best theories for dealing with the chaos in the lives of people. This Chaos Theory was developed in the 1970s when James Gleick and Edward Lorenz found that small changes and fateful events set off patterns that could affect everything in the surroundings. They referred to this as the "butterfly effect" when they observed that a butterfly flapping its wings in China could affect weather patterns in Europe.

Therefore, even though chaos finds its way into the lives of every person, it is critical that people find ways to effectively cope with and overcome the chaos. The Chaos Theory suggests that there is no chaos; rather, there is a pattern and underlying order that can be defined by observing it with the right lens.

The purpose of this book is to provide people with the right lens to see the patterns in the chaos in their lives. This workbook will show participants that although chaos can be frustrating and stressful, by being redirected it can also enrich lives and provide a sense of meaning and purpose.

**In this book, we will illustrate several ways to embrace and manage chaos:**

- **Expect it** – In the twenty-first century it is almost impossible to avoid chaos in life. People need to be aware that their plans are likely to be interrupted and changed, and that everything cannot be predicted and controlled.

- **Understand it** – By seeing chaos for what it is and accepting and controlling it, people can see chaos as freedom from predictable routines and constraints. Eventually, chaos can be seen as a transition point to a more controlled, calm and satisfying life.

- **See it for what it is** – Chaos Theory reminds people that even in chaos one can find distinct, critical life patterns. When people are able to identify the patterns in their lives, they can work to control the chaos and live simpler lives.

- **Control It** – Chaos Theory suggests that there is always going to be chaos in the lives of most people. The secret is to be alert to the opportunities chaos brings and find ways of doing one's best to control it so that it does not negatively affect one's life.

All people at some point will experience chaos that will come from a wide variety of sources and can cause people to feel frustrated, stressed out and weary. Most people see this chaos as a symptom of the twenty-first century and feel that there is nothing they can do about it. In reality, chaos can be seen for what it is. People can do something about it and control it in their own lives.

To lead a more stress-free, calm and satisfying life, it is important to deal with the emotions, thoughts and actions related to chaos. The *Coping with Chaos Workbook* provides assessments and self-guided activities to help participants learn useful skills for coping with various forms of chaos. Self-exploration activities are provided for participants to determine which best suit their unique needs.

# Format of Book

The *Coping with Chaos Workbook* contains assessments and guided self-exploration to use with a variety of populations to help participants cope more effectively with chaos in their lives. Each chapter of this workbook begins with a Table of Contents annotated with notes and examples for the facilitator. Each chapter contains two primary elements: 1) a set of assessments to help participants gather information about themselves in a focused situation, and 2) a set of guided self-exploration activities to help participants process information and learn ways of coping with chaos.

## Assessments

Each chapter begins with an assessment that provides participants with valuable information about themselves. These assessments help identify productive and unproductive patterns of behavior and life skills, and they encourage development of an awareness of ways to interact with the world. Assessments provide a path to self-discovery through participants' exploration of their own unique traits and behaviors. The purpose of these assessments is not to "pigeon-hole" people, but to allow them to explore various elements critical for coping with guilt and shame. This book contains *self-assessments* and not *tests*. Traditional tests measure knowledge or right or wrong responses. For the assessments provided in this book, remind participants that there are no right or wrong answers. These assessments ask only for opinions or attitudes about topics related to a variety of coping skills and abilities.

The assessments in this book are based on self-reported data. In other words, the accuracy and usefulness of the information is dependent on the information that participants honestly provide about themselves. All of the assessments in this workbook are designed to be administered, scored, and interpreted by the participants as a starting point for them to begin to learn more about themselves and their coping skills. Remind participants that the assessments are exploratory exercises and not a determination of abilities. Lastly, the assessments are not a substitute for professional assistance. If you feel any of your participants need more assistance than you can provide, please refer them to an appropriate professional.

**As your participants begin the assessments in this workbook give these instructions:**

- Take your time. Because there is no time limit for completing the assessments, work at your own pace. Allow yourself time to reflect on your results and how they compare to what you already know about yourself.

- Do not answer the assessments as you think others would like you to answer them or how you think others see you. These assessments are for you to reflect on your life and explore some of the barriers that are keeping you from living a calmer, more rational and less anxious life.

- Assessments are powerful tools if you are honest with yourself. Take your time and be truthful in your responses so that your results are an honest reflection of *you*. Your level of commitment in completing the assessments honestly will determine how much you learn about yourself.

- Before completing each assessment, be sure to read the instructions. The assessments have similar formats, but they have different scales, responses, scoring instructions and methods for interpretation.

- Finally, remember that learning about yourself should be a positive and motivating experience. Don't stress about taking the assessments or discovering your results. Just respond honestly and learn as much about yourself as you can.

*(Continued on the next page)*

## Format of Book (Continued)

### Guided Self-Exploration Activities

Guided self-exploration activities are any exercises that assist participants in self-reflection and enhance self-knowledge, identify potential ineffective behaviors, and teach more effective ways of coping. Guided self-exploration is designed to help participants make a series of discoveries that lead to increased social and emotional competencies, as well as to serve as an energizing way to help participants grow personally and professionally. These brief, easy-to-use self-reflection tools are designed to promote insight and self-growth. Many different types of guided self-exploration activities are provided for you to pick and chose the activities most needed and/or will be most appealing to the participants. The unique features of self-guided exploration activities make them usable and appropriate for a variety of individual sessions and group sessions.

### Features of Guided Self-Exploration Activities

Quick, easy and rewarding to use – These guided self-exploration activities are designed to be an efficient, appealing method for motivating participants to explore information about themselves - including their thoughts, feelings, and behaviors - in a relatively short period of time.

- **Reproducible** – Because the guided self-exploration activities can be reproduced by the facilitator, no more than the one book needs to be purchased. You may photocopy as many items as you wish for your participants. If you want to add or delete words on a page, make one photocopy, white out and/or write your own words, and then make photocopies from your personalized master.

- **Participative** – These guided self-exploration activities help people to quickly focus their attention in the self-reflection process and to learn new and more effective ways of coping.

- **Motivating to complete** – The guided self-exploration activities are designed to be an energizing way for participants to engage in self-reflection and learn about themselves. Various activities are included to enhance the learning process related to developing important social and emotional competency skills.

- **Low risk** – The guided self-exploration activities are designed to be less risky than formal assessments and structured exercises. They are user-friendly, and participants will generally feel rewarded and motivated after completing these activities.

- **Adaptable to a variety of populations** – The guided self-exploration activities can be used with many different populations and can be tailored to meet the needs of the specific populations with whom you work.

- **Focused** – Each guided self-exploration activity is designed to focus on a single coping issue, thus enhancing the experience for participants.

- **Flexible** – The guided self-exploration activities are flexible and can be used independently or to supplement other types of interventions.

# Chapter Elements

The *Coping with Chaos Workbook* is designed to be used either independently or as part of an integrated curriculum. You may administer any of the assessments and the guided self-exploration activities to an individual or a group with whom you are working, or you may administer any of the activities over one or more days. Feel free to pick and choose those assessments and activities that best fit the outcomes you desire.

**The first page of each chapter begins with a Table of Contents annotated with ideas and examples for the facilitator.**

**Assessments** – Assessments with scoring directions and interpretation materials begin each chapter. The authors recommend that you begin presenting each topic by asking participants to complete the assessment. Facilitators can choose one or more, or all of the activities relevant to their participants' specific needs and concerns.

**Guided Self-Exploration Activities** – Practical questions and activities to prompt self-reflection and promote self-understanding are included after each of the assessments. These questions and activities foster introspection and promote pro-social behaviors and coping skills. The activities in this workbook are tied to the assessments so that you can identify and select activities quickly and easily.

The activities are divided into four chapters to help you identify and select assessments easily and quickly:

- **Chapter 1: Disorganization**
  This chapter helps participants explore how a lack of organization in personal and professional life leads to feeling a sense of chaos.
- **Chapter 2: Control of Chaos**
  This chapter helps participants explore how well they are able to control the effects of chaos in their lives through limiting distractions, staying organized, and maintaining influence of their lives despite outside forces.
- **Chapter 3: Juggling Multiple Roles**
  This chapter helps participants explore their effectiveness in juggling multiple roles and finding balance among the roles they play.
- **Chapter 4: Time-Pressure**
  This chapter helps participants identify and explore the impact that poor time management skills is having on their overall level of life chaos.

## *Thanks to . . .*

**Amy Brodsky, illustrator extraordinaire,**

and to the following professionals whose input in this book has been invaluable!

Jay Leutenberg

Kathy Liptak, Ed.D.

Eileen Regen, M.Ed., CJE

Coping with Chaos Introduction

# Table of Contents

## Disorganization
Facilitator's Annotated Table of Contents . . . . . . . . . . . . . 11–12
Disorganization Introduction and Directions. . . . . . . . . . . . . . 13
Disorganization Scale . . . . . . . . . . . . . . . . . . . . . . . . 14–15
Scoring Directions. . . . . . . . . . . . . . . . . . . . . . . . . . . . 16
Profile Interpretation . . . . . . . . . . . . . . . . . . . . . . . . . . 16
Declutter Your Life . . . . . . . . . . . . . . . . . . . . . . . . . . . 17
My Master To Do List . . . . . . . . . . . . . . . . . . . . . . . . . . 18
Learning to Say "No" . . . . . . . . . . . . . . . . . . . . . . . . . . 19
To Toss or Not to Toss. . . . . . . . . . . . . . . . . . . . . . . . . . 20
Organize Your Space. . . . . . . . . . . . . . . . . . . . . . . . . . . 21
Simplify Where and When . . . . . . . . . . . . . . . . . . . . . . . 22
What They Look Like . . . . . . . . . . . . . . . . . . . . . . . . . . 23
Delegating Responsibilities at Home. . . . . . . . . . . . . . . . . . 24
Delegating Responsibilities at Work . . . . . . . . . . . . . . . . . . 25
Organizing Myself. . . . . . . . . . . . . . . . . . . . . . . . . . . . 26
My Goals . . . . . . . . . . . . . . . . . . . . . . . . . . . . . . . . . 27
Organizing Made Easy . . . . . . . . . . . . . . . . . . . . . . . . . 28
What's Your Organizational Style?. . . . . . . . . . . . . . . . . . . 29
Getting Your Life Organized. . . . . . . . . . . . . . . . . . . . . . 30

## Control of Chaos
Facilitator's Annotated Table of Contents . . . . . . . . . . . . . 31–32
Control of Chaos Introduction and Directions . . . . . . . . . . . . 33
Control of Chaos Scale. . . . . . . . . . . . . . . . . . . . . . . . . . 34
Scoring Directions. . . . . . . . . . . . . . . . . . . . . . . . . . . . 35
Profile Interpretation . . . . . . . . . . . . . . . . . . . . . . . . . . 35
Calm in My Life. . . . . . . . . . . . . . . . . . . . . . . . . . . . . . 36
Frenzy in My Life at Home. . . . . . . . . . . . . . . . . . . . . . . 37
The Frenzy with My Work or Volunteering . . . . . . . . . . . . . . 38
What Chaos Looks Like to Me . . . . . . . . . . . . . . . . . . . . . 39
Chaos Metaphors . . . . . . . . . . . . . . . . . . . . . . . . . . . . 40
Steps to Conquer Chaos . . . . . . . . . . . . . . . . . . . . . . . . 41
Bring Order to Your Life . . . . . . . . . . . . . . . . . . . . . . . . 42
Feng Shui. . . . . . . . . . . . . . . . . . . . . . . . . . . . . . . . . 43
Type-A Personality . . . . . . . . . . . . . . . . . . . . . . . . . . . 44
Find a Place for Everything and Put Everything in Its Place. . . . 45
Wearing Many Hats. . . . . . . . . . . . . . . . . . . . . . . . . . . 46
Superhero Syndrome . . . . . . . . . . . . . . . . . . . . . . . . . . 47
Overcoming Technological Distractions . . . . . . . . . . . . . . . 48
My Chaos Letter . . . . . . . . . . . . . . . . . . . . . . . . . . . . . 49
Stillness Inside You . . . . . . . . . . . . . . . . . . . . . . . . . . . 50

# Table of Contents *(continued)*

## Juggling Multiple Roles

| | |
|---|---|
| Facilitator's Annotated Table of Contents | 51–52 |
| Juggling Multiple Roles Scale Introduction and Directions | 53 |
| Juggling Multiple Roles Scale | 54 |
| Scoring Directions | 55 |
| Profile Interpretation | 55 |
| Expectations of Others | 56 |
| Expectations of Myself | 57 |
| Time Spent in My Roles | 58 |
| Changes in My Roles | 59 |
| Set Boundaries | 60 |
| Put Myself First | 61 |
| Taking on New Roles | 62 |
| Shedding Unwanted Roles | 63 |
| What are My Values | 64 |
| Prioritizing My Roles | 65 |
| Delegating | 66 |
| Choices, Choices, Choices | 67 |
| Consequences of Role Overload | 68 |
| My Ideal Word Script | 69 |
| Chaos to the World Brings Uneasiness, but | 70 |

## Time-Pressure

| | |
|---|---|
| Facilitator's Annotated Table of Contents | 71–72 |
| Time-Pressure Scale Introduction and Directions | 73 |
| Time-Pressure Scale | 74–75 |
| Scoring Directions | 76 |
| Profile Interpretation | 76 |
| Negative Time-Pressure Behaviors | 77 |
| Feelings When Facing Too Much Time-Pressure | 78 |
| What I Procrastinate About | 79 |
| Time Caricatures | 80 |
| Reasons I Procrastinate | 81 |
| My Time Clock | 82 |
| Time Slips Away at Home | 83 |
| Time Slips Away at Work or Other Places | 84 |
| Time Fears | 85 |
| Slow Down! | 86 |
| I Feel Driven | 87 |
| Multitasking | 88 |
| My Involuntary Obligations | 89 |
| Changing My Involuntary Obligations | 90 |

# Disorganization

## Table of Contents and Facilitator Notes

Disorganization Introduction and Directions . . . . . . . . . . . . . 13
Disorganization Scale . . . . . . . . . . . . . . . . . . . . . . . . . 14–15
Scoring Directions . . . . . . . . . . . . . . . . . . . . . . . . . . . 16
Profile Interpretation . . . . . . . . . . . . . . . . . . . . . . . . . 16
De-clutter Your Life . . . . . . . . . . . . . . . . . . . . . . . . . . 17

*EXAMPLE:*

| Item | Why I Keep It | Why I Think I Can Toss It or Give It Away |
|---|---|---|
| Ex: old computer printer | In case mine breaks | It is not compatible with my current computer. |

My Master To Do List . . . . . . . . . . . . . . . . . . . . . . . . . 18

*EXAMPLE:*

| Need to Do at Home | Completion Date |
|---|---|
| Ex: I need to clean out my garage. | June 1 |

Learning to Say "No" . . . . . . . . . . . . . . . . . . . . . . . . . 19

*EXAMPLE:*

| Person to Whom I Can't Say No | Tasks I Am Asked to Do | How I Can Say No in a Polite and Assertive Way |
|---|---|---|
| Ex: My friend Sherry | She often asks me to get the mail for her even though it is one of her responsibilities. | Sherry, I don't mind helping you with the mail if it's an emergency, but mail delivery is one of your responsibilities. |

To Toss or not to Toss . . . . . . . . . . . . . . . . . . . . . . . . . 20

*EXAMPLE:*

| Item | Location | Why I Have Kept It |
|---|---|---|
| Stack of old magazines | Coffee table | To look at recipes later |

*After participants have completed the activity, remind them to clean up their computer desktops.*

Organize Your Space . . . . . . . . . . . . . . . . . . . . . . . . . 21

*Suggest that participants begin with the area(s) of their life and career that are the least organized.*

Disorganization

## Table of Contents and Facilitator Notes

### Simplify Where and When Possible .................................22

| Item | Location | Why It Is Okay to Dispose of It |
|---|---|---|
| Clothing collection | Bedroom closet | Have not worn those clothes for years and I can give them to the needy. |

### What They Look Like ...............................................23
*Ask for a volunteer to write about or draw on the board what he/she thinks organization and disorganization looks like to her/him. Then, distribute handout.*

### Delegating Responsibilities at Home ..............................24
*After the participants have completed the handout, ask for volunteers willing to share what they would like to delegate to make their lives less chaotic.*

### Delegating Responsibilities at Work...............................25
*After the participants have completed the handout, ask for volunteers willing to share what they would like to delegate to make their lives less chaotic.*

### Organizing Myself................................................26
*Ask for volunteers to define what the phrase 'organizing myself' means to them personally. Then distribute handouts.*

### My Goals........................................................27
*Prior to distributing handouts, ask the group to define goals and how they help people. After some discussion, share the following definition: Goals give your life purpose and direction, and they serve to motivate you.*

### Organizing Made Easy ...........................................28
*After handouts have been completed, ask for volunteers who would like to share and read their ideas.*

### What's Your Organizational Style? ...............................29
*After the participants have completed the handout, ask people to break off into Organizational Style groups to discuss their style and how they feel it works for them. Ask a representative of each group to announce to everyone their group's consensus.*

### Getting Your Life Organized......................................30
*After handout is completed, ask for a show of hands of people who already use the first suggestion on the page. Ask for someone to talk about it. Proceed with each of the suggestions on the page.*

# Disorganization Scale
# Introduction and Directions

When you think of stress, you probably think of major life transitions such as losing your job, caring for an aging or ill parent, mourning the loss of a loved one, or experiencing a significant financial loss. Often it isn't the big stressors that cause chaos, but little stressors adding up. A lack of organization in your personal and professional life will keep you feeling that sense of chaos.

For each of the items that follow, choose the response that best describes you. In the following example, the circled numbers indicate how much the statement is descriptive of the person completing the inventory.

**3 = Very Much Like Me    2 = A Little Like Me    1 = Not At All Like Me**

## When I am at work . . .

1. I have too much to do . . . . . . . . . . . . . . . . . . . . . . . . . . . 3   (2)   1
2. I do not prioritize my work efficiently . . . . . . . . . . . . . . . . . (3)   2   1

This is not a test. Since there are no right or wrong answers, do not spend too much time thinking about your answers. Be sure to respond to every statement.

*Turn to the next page and begin.*

Disorganization

# Disorganization Scale

## I. Organization at Work

*(Work in this case can be a part-time job, full-time job, volunteer experience, home business or any other situation in which you do a job.)*

**3 = Very Much Like Me     2 = A Little Like Me     1 = Not At All Like Me**

### When I am at work . . .

| | | | |
|---|---|---|---|
| 1. I have too much to do | 3 | 2 | 1 |
| 2. I do not prioritize my work efficiently | 3 | 2 | 1 |
| 3. I feel overloaded with things I don't like to do | 3 | 2 | 1 |
| 4. I have trouble managing my time | 3 | 2 | 1 |
| 5. I can't keep up with the changes | 3 | 2 | 1 |
| 6. I have a difficult time saying "no" to co-workers | 3 | 2 | 1 |
| 7. I tend to be a perfectionist | 3 | 2 | 1 |
| 8. I don't use a To Do List | 3 | 2 | 1 |
| 9. I have too many unwanted interruptions | 3 | 2 | 1 |
| 10. I don't make the time to take breaks | 3 | 2 | 1 |
| 11. I do not use a planner to manage my time | 3 | 2 | 1 |
| 12. I am not as productive as I should be and it frustrates me | 3 | 2 | 1 |
| 13. I have trouble keeping track of what I need to do | 3 | 2 | 1 |
| 14. I don't put things away, so I don't know where they are | 3 | 2 | 1 |
| 15. I rarely delegate tasks to others | 3 | 2 | 1 |

**I. TOTAL = _____**

*Continued on the next page*

# Disorganization Scale *Continued*

## II. Organization at Home

*(Home in this case is the time you spend at home alone or with others living in the home.)*

**3 = Very Much Like Me    2 = A Little Like Me    1 = Not At All Like Me**

### When I am at home . . .

| | | | |
|---|---|---|---|
| 1. I have too much to do | 3 | 2 | 1 |
| 2. I do not prioritize my tasks efficiently | 3 | 2 | 1 |
| 3. I feel overloaded with things I don't like to do. | 3 | 2 | 1 |
| 4. I have trouble managing my time | 3 | 2 | 1 |
| 5. I can't keep up with the changes | 3 | 2 | 1 |
| 6. I have a difficult time saying "no" to others | 3 | 2 | 1 |
| 7. I tend to be a perfectionist | 3 | 2 | 1 |
| 8. I don't use a To Do List | 3 | 2 | 1 |
| 9. I have too many unwanted interruptions | 3 | 2 | 1 |
| 10. I don't make the time to take breaks | 3 | 2 | 1 |
| 11. I do not use a planner to manage my time | 3 | 2 | 1 |
| 12. I am not as productive as I should be and it frustrates me | 3 | 2 | 1 |
| 13. I have trouble keeping track of what I need to do | 3 | 2 | 1 |
| 14. I don't put things away, so I don't know where they are | 3 | 2 | 1 |
| 15. I rarely delegate tasks to others | 3 | 2 | 1 |

**II. TOTAL = _____**

*Go to the Scoring Directions on the next page*

Disorganization

# Disorganization Scale
# Scoring Directions

The Disorganization Scale is designed to measure how organized or disorganized you are at work and at home. For each of the sections, count the scores you circled for each of the two sections. Put that total on the line marked "Total" at the end of each section.

Then, transfer your totals to the spaces below.

**TOTAL I.** _____  =  **Organization at Work**

**TOTAL II.** _____  =  **Organization at Home**

# Profile Interpretation

| Scales Scores | Result | Indications |
|---|---|---|
| **Scores from 36 to 45** | High | If you score in the high range, you often feel very disorganized in that environment. |
| **Scores from 25 to 35** | Moderate | If you score in the moderate range, you sometimes feel disorganized in that environment. |
| **Scores from 15 to 24** | Low | If you score in the low range, you feel fairly organized in that environment. |

By developing your organizational skills, you will begin to experience less chaos in your life. The following exercises are designed to help you become better organized at both work and home.

Disorganization

# De-clutter Your Life

Many people hang onto things that they do not really need.
What types of objects have you acquired over the years that you no longer need?
List objects at home or work that you could easily give or throw away.
(You can toss these, sell them, or give these items to a charitable cause.)

Think about the following questions in deciding what to dispose of:
- Do I need this item?
- Will I miss it if I don't have it? How much?
- Have I used it in the last year?
- Will I need it next year?

| Item | Why I Keep it | Why I Think I Can Toss it or Give it Away |
|---|---|---|
|  |  |  |
|  |  |  |
|  |  |  |
|  |  |  |
|  |  |  |
|  |  |  |
|  |  |  |
|  |  |  |
|  |  |  |
|  |  |  |

**From the list above, what adds to the clutter in your life?**

_____

_____

_____

Disorganization

## My Master To Do List

Do you keep a master to-do list of tasks that need to be accomplished for the week? If not, now is the time to begin doing so. In the spaces that follow, list the things you need to do at home and at work, and set a date for it to be completed.

### Home

| Need to Do at Home | Completion Date |
|---|---|
|  |  |
|  |  |
|  |  |
|  |  |
|  |  |
|  |  |
|  |  |

### Work

| Need to Do at work | Completion Date |
|---|---|
|  |  |
|  |  |
|  |  |
|  |  |
|  |  |
|  |  |
|  |  |

Disorganization

# Learning to Say "No"

Often requests come from people at home or at work that are hard to turn down.
By doing so, you add to the long list of tasks that already occupy your time.
It will be helpful to say *no* to tasks that will occupy too much of your time.
List the people to whom you have difficulty saying no and the types of tasks that they
ask of you. Then think of a way to assertively and politely say *no*.

| Person to whom I Can't say *No* | Tasks I Am Asked to Do | How I Can Say *No* in a Polite and Assertive Way |
|---|---|---|
| | | |
| | | |
| | | |
| | | |
| | | |
| | | |
| | | |

From the list above, what adds to the clutter in your life?

_____

_____

Disorganization

## To Toss or Not To Toss?

When you attempt to organize your desk area at home and/or your office you probably feel you are wasting your time and get frustrated. It's time to rid yourself of unwanted notes, files, pieces of paper, catalogues, letters, mail, advertisements and other paper products. To get started, think about the items you don't need, but still keep.

| Item | Location | Why I Have Kept It |
|------|----------|--------------------|
|      |          |                    |
|      |          |                    |
|      |          |                    |
|      |          |                    |
|      |          |                    |
|      |          |                    |
|      |          |                    |
|      |          |                    |
|      |          |                    |
|      |          |                    |
|      |          |                    |
|      |          |                    |

**Computer Recycling Bin**

Now that you have rid yourself of those unwanted papers it is time to do the same with your technology. Begin by cleaning up your computer. Delete your old, outdated, unwanted folders, shortcuts and individual documents. When your computer is better organized, you will find that your stress-level will go down, especially when you need to find something on your computer.

# Organize Your Space

Organizing your space, wherever it is, will make such a difference! Try it!

| My Space | How I Can Organize it | How I Would Benefit |
|---|---|---|
| Car | | |
| Closets | | |
| Computer | | |
| Desk | | |
| Garage | | |
| Home | | |
| Kitchen | | |
| Office | | |
| Other | | |

Disorganization

# Simplify Where and When Possible

In what ways can you simplify your life?
One method is to dispose of those things that are not essential.
In the spaces that follow, list the items you want to get rid of, where each is located (closet, garage, kitchen, etc.), and how disposing of it will make your life less chaotic.

| Item | Location | Why It Is Okay to Dispose of It |
|------|----------|-------------------------------|
|      |          |                               |
|      |          |                               |
|      |          |                               |
|      |          |                               |
|      |          |                               |
|      |          |                               |
|      |          |                               |
|      |          |                               |
|      |          |                               |
|      |          |                               |
|      |          |                               |

# What They Look Like

Draw or write about what you think disorganization and organization look like.

| **Disorganization** |
|---|
| |

| **Organization** |
|---|
| |

## Delegating Responsibilities at Home

It is helpful to delegate some of your responsibilities to others in your home.
Your success will depend on choosing the right person to do the right task,
to ensure it being done well and the person being willing to do it.

| Tasks I Can Delegate | To Whom I Will Delegate | How This Will Free My Time |
|---|---|---|
|  |  |  |
|  |  |  |
|  |  |  |
|  |  |  |
|  |  |  |
|  |  |  |
|  |  |  |
|  |  |  |

Disorganization

## Delegating Responsibilities at Work

It is often helpful if you can delegate some of your responsibilities to others at work. Your success will depend on choosing the right person to do the right task, to ensure it being done well and the person being willing to do it.

| Tasks I Can Delegate | To Whom I Will Delegate | How This Will Free My Time |
|---|---|---|
| | | |
| | | |
| | | |
| | | |
| | | |
| | | |
| | | |
| | | |

Disorganization

# Organizing Myself

By keeping a running list of *things to do, places to go and calls to make* each day,
as well as *what needs to happen tomorrow*,
you will be able to stay on top of everything without being overwhelmed.

### Things I Must Do

1. _____
2. _____
3. _____
4. _____
5. _____
6. _____
7. _____
8. _____

### Places I Need to Go

1. _____
2. _____
3. _____
4. _____
5. _____
6. _____
7. _____
8. _____

### Calls I Need to Make

1. _____
2. _____
3. _____
4. _____
5. _____
6. _____
7. _____
8. _____

### Things to Do tomorrow

1. _____
2. _____
3. _____
4. _____
5. _____
6. _____
7. _____
8. _____

Disorganization

# My Goals

Setting goals can help you be more organized,
and writing them down can be your biggest time saver.
Goals give your life purpose and direction, and serve to motivate you.

What are your goals in the following areas?

Career _____

_____

Community _____

_____

Family _____

_____

Financial _____

_____

Friendships _____

_____

Home _____

_____

Leisure _____

_____

Mental Health _____

_____

Personal Relationships _____

_____

Physical Health _____

_____

Spiritual or Religious Life _____

_____

Disorganization

# Organizing Made Easy

How can you stop procrastinating and become organized to accomplish more? The method below has been used successfully to help people become more organized.

A needed project in my home or office is _____

Start where you can accomplish the most. You don't need to start at the beginning, just the place that needs the most organization. Here is how/where I will start: _____
_____
_____
_____
_____
_____

To get this project done, my To Do List includes the following: _____
_____
_____
_____
_____
_____
_____

Being realistic, this project will take me _____
_____

Once I get started, it will take me this much time to finish: _____

I will make a commitment to begin on _____
　　　　　　　　　　　　　　　　　　　　　　　　　　DAY/DATE

After I have finished I will reward myself for a job well done by _____
_____
_____

# What's Your Organization Style?

There are many ways that people remain organized (or disorganized).
Most people are a combination of several of these types.
Look at the following organizational types, and for each one,
describe the types of items you organize in each particular style.

**Sorter** – This type of person carefully categorizes items and then files them away where they belong.

What types of items do you sort?

_____

_____

_____

**Stacker** – This type of person creates organized piles of items.

What types of items do you stack?

_____

_____

_____

**Stuffer** – This type of person shoves unsorted papers into a drawer or file folders to be handled at a later date.

What types of items do you stuff?

_____

_____

_____

**Slinger** – This type of person simply slings items anywhere and everywhere.

What types of items do you sling?

_____

_____

_____

Disorganization

# Getting Your Life Organized

Following are some of the ways in which you can get your life organized.
Place a ✔ (check mark in the box) by those that you already do.
Then place a * (star) behind those you need to do.

- ❑ Ask for help if you need it
- ❑ Assign a place for everything
- ❑ Avoid trying to be perfect
- ❑ Clean out the drawers in your kitchen
- ❑ Clear your house of clutter
- ❑ Create a filing system for important papers
- ❑ Delegate
- ❑ Do one thing at a time
- ❑ Find ways to cope with stress
- ❑ Eliminate negative self-talk
- ❑ Enter important documents in a 3-ring binder
- ❑ Gather less stuff
- ❑ Have a phone book in the car
- ❑ Insert a complete check list in your exercise bag or back-pack
- ❑ Keep and use a planner
- ❑ Leave only everyday items on your desk
- ❑ Make check list for items to take on trip
- ❑ Manage your time well
- ❑ Merge like things together (rags and cleaning products)
- ❑ Multi-task effectively
- ❑ Organize your space
- ❑ Place a wastebasket in every room
- ❑ Practice prioritizing tasks
- ❑ Put things away
- ❑ Rely on "to-do" lists
- ❑ Say "no" if you have to
- ❑ Schedule standing appointments
- ❑ Simplify where possible
- ❑ Stash cleaning supplies in a plastic caddy
- ❑ Stop procrastinating
- ❑ Take time-out if you need it
- ❑ Throw unneeded clothing, shoes and household items in a handy charity box
- ❑ Toss the junk mail
- ❑ Use post-it notes
- ❑ Work on keeping everything in its place
- ❑ Write things down

# Control of Chaos

## Table of Contents and Facilitator Notes

**Control of Chaos Introduction and Directions** . . . . . . . . . . . .33
**Control of Chaos Scale** . . . . . . . . . . . . . . . . . . . . . . . . . . . .34
**Scoring Directions** . . . . . . . . . . . . . . . . . . . . . . . . . . . . . . .35
**Profile Interpretation** . . . . . . . . . . . . . . . . . . . . . . . . . . . . .35
**Calm in My Life**. . . . . . . . . . . . . . . . . . . . . . . . . . . . . . . . . . .36

*After participants have completed the handout, ask volunteers to share some of the times in life when remaining calm was very important. Ask for a show of hands of people who have had the same experience. Then ask for a show of hands of those who may be willing to try the calming strategy described. Continue with another volunteer and another strategy to stay calm.*

**Frenzy in My Life at Home** . . . . . . . . . . . . . . . . . . . . . . . . .37

*Ask if any participants are willing to share an instance of a time when their life is frenzied at home.*

**The Frenzy with My Work or Volunteering**. . . . . . . . . . . . . .38

*Ask if any participants are willing to share an instance of when their life is frenzied at work.*

**What Chaos Looks Like to Me** . . . . . . . . . . . . . . . . . . . . . .39

*After participants complete their drawings, doodling, or sketches, ask for permission to tape them to the wall for show and tell. It is okay if someone passes.*

**Chaos Metaphors** . . . . . . . . . . . . . . . . . . . . . . . . . . . . . . . .40

*Ask participants for their definitions of a metaphor. After several have shared, provide the following definition: A metaphor is a statement that compares two objects that are otherwise unrelated. For example, chaos is a tornado in my life. Distribute handouts.*

**Steps to Conquer Chaos** . . . . . . . . . . . . . . . . . . . . . . . . . .41

*Prior to participants completing the handout, ask four participants to read one of the steps, beginning with the step on top. Follow each one by reading the following examples in italics.*

Feel like you are in control: *I am going to be more organized.*
Begin ordering items: *I will begin by organizing the garage, then I will move to the house.*
Limit Distractions: *I will keep the door closed so the neighbors don't distract me.*
Move on: *I will throw away things I don't need.*

**Bringing Order to Your Life** . . . . . . . . . . . . . . . . . . . . . . . . 42
EXAMPLE:

| Area of My Life | What and Who Causes Chaos | What and Who Promotes Calm |
|---|---|---|
| My family | My partner is unkind to my children (they are not his kids). I feel I am always in the middle. | At work, my co-workers and boss are supportive and I love my work. I can forget for a while when I'm there. |

© 2013 WHOLE PERSON ASSOCIATES, 101 WEST 2ND ST., SUITE 203, DULUTH MN 55802 • 800-247-6789

# Control of Chaos

## Table of Contents and Facilitator Notes

### Feng Shui...........................................43
*Discuss with participants the definition of Feng Shui. If you have pictures of examples of Feng Shui, pass them around. Ask them to share how they re-arranged their living space so that it is less cluttered and in greater harmony.*

### Type-A Personality.................................44
*Ask participants what they believe are some of the characteristics of a person with a Type-A Personality.*

*After completion of the handout, see how many traits the group was able to generate. Ask for a show of hands of Type-A personality people.*

### Find a Place for Everything and Put Everything in its Place...45
Example:

| Items that Need a Place | Where You Can Put Items to Find them Easily |
|---|---|
| My mail | I will put a box with file folders on my kitchen desk. I'll make a file for bills to pay, a file for things I need to take care of right away and another file for things to do later. |

### Wearing Many Hats................................46
*Discuss the reasons people today wear so many hats. Talk about the positive and negative aspects of wearing many hats.*

### Superhero Syndrome..............................47
*Ask for volunteers, one by one, to name a Superhero and what this person can do that they would like to be able to do. Take a vote on which Superhero they would like to be. Then, distribute the handout.*

### Overcoming Technology Distractions................48
*After completing the handouts, ask for volunteers to share some of the ways they are willing to reduce the distraction of technology in their lives.*

### My Chaos Letter..................................49
*Prior to distributing handout, remind participants that this letter is cathartic, as well as a method to provide insight into ways to begin reducing the chaos in life.*

### Stillness Inside You...............................50
*Suggest to participants who related to this quotation that they cut it out and post it in a place where they will see it often.*

# Control of Chaos
# Introduction and Directions

Some people are able to control the effects of chaos better than others. These people tend to believe in their ability to influence their lives more than outside forces, stay organized, and be good at limiting distractions.

This assessment contains 30 statements related to three important behaviors necessary in control chaos in your life. Read each of the statements and decide whether or not the statement describes you. If the statement does describe you, circle the number under the YES column next to that item. If the statement does not describe you, circle the number under the NO column next to that item.

In the following example, the circled number under "Yes" indicates the statement is descriptive of the person completing the inventory.

|  | YES | NO |
|---|---|---|
| I am the master of my own destiny | (2) | 1 |

This is not a test. Since there are no right or wrong answers, do not spend too much time thinking about your answers. Your initial response will be the most true for you.
Be sure to respond to every statement.

*Turn to the next page and begin.*

# Control of Chaos Scale

|  | YES | NO |
|---|---|---|
| **C.** | | |
| I am the master of my own destiny | 2 | 1 |
| I find it difficult to control the chaos in my life | 1 | 2 |
| I determine the course of my life | 2 | 1 |
| When I make a plan, I am certain to make it work | 2 | 1 |
| I am often the victim of forces I cannot understand | 1 | 2 |
| I trust my life to fate | 1 | 2 |
| Heredity determines people's success | 1 | 2 |
| I believe that what is going to happen will happen, no matter what | 1 | 2 |
| People cannot change basic behavior patterns | 1 | 2 |
| Luck has nothing to do with being successful | 2 | 1 |

C. TOTAL _____

|  | YES | NO |
|---|---|---|
| **O.** | | |
| I often am absentminded | 1 | 2 |
| I often forget where I put things | 1 | 2 |
| I tend not to have too much clutter in my life | 2 | 1 |
| I have a hard time focusing on matters at hand | 1 | 2 |
| I am usually on time, not late | 2 | 1 |
| I never get ahead when trying to keep up with the demands on my time | 1 | 2 |
| I am stressed out by the disorganization in my life | 1 | 2 |
| I believe I am fairly efficient | 2 | 1 |
| I feel like I'm on the brink of chaos at all times | 1 | 2 |
| My life is running fairly smoothly | 2 | 1 |

O. TOTAL _____

|  | YES | NO |
|---|---|---|
| **D.** | | |
| I do not let social media sites take me away from what I am doing | 2 | 1 |
| I am easily distracted | 1 | 2 |
| I have trouble paying attention to the present moment | 1 | 2 |
| I make excuses not to finish tasks | 1 | 2 |
| I easily lose focus when I am doing something | 1 | 2 |
| I have eliminated many distractions from my life | 2 | 1 |
| I allow other people to draw me away from my work | 1 | 2 |
| I block sites that distract me on the Internet | 2 | 1 |
| I am often side-tracked by e-mails and other technologies | 1 | 2 |
| I find myself surfing the Internet rather than working | 1 | 2 |

D. TOTAL _____

*Go to the Scoring Directions on the next page*

# Control of Chaos Scale
# Scoring Directions

The ability to control chaos lies on the continuum of being very much in control to having no or limited control.

For the sections you just completed, add the numbers that you circled which are indicated in the C Section. This will give you your Control score, which will range from 10 to 20. Place that number in the space below marked (C) Control Total.
Do the same for the other two scales: (O) Order Total and (D) Distractions Total.
Then, transfer those totals to the spaces below:

(C) Control Total = _____

(O) Order Total = _____

(D) Distractions Total = _____

To get your overall Control Total, add the three scores above.
Total scores range from 30 to 60.
Put that score in the space provided below.

**CONTROL OF CHAOS TOTAL** = _____

# Profile Interpretation

| Individual Scale Score | Total Scales Score | Result | Indications |
|---|---|---|---|
| Scores from 10 to 13 | Scores from 30 to 39 | Low | Low scores indicate that you are rarely able to control the chaos in your life. |
| Scores from 14 to 17 | Scores from 40 to 50 | Moderate | Moderate scores indicate that you can sometimes control the chaos in your life. You still need to do more. |
| Scores from 18 to 20 | Scores from 51 to 60 | High | High scores indicate that you often are able to control the chaos in your life. |

Complete the following exercises to build chaos-control resources.

Control of Chaos

# Calm in My Life

It is important to identify the times in your life when you are calm. List the times in your life when you are the calmest, what you are doing at the time, and what usually interrupts your moments of calm.

| Times I Am Calm | What I Am Doing | What Interrupts My Calm |
|---|---|---|
|  |  |  |
|  |  |  |
|  |  |  |
|  |  |  |
|  |  |  |
|  |  |  |

What patterns do you see? _____

_____

_____

Control of Chaos

# Frenzy in My Life at Home

It is important to identify when you find yourself becoming frenzied at home.

List the situation that is happening, with whom, and what you can do to make it better.

| Situation | With Whom | What I Can Do to Reduce the Frenzy |
|---|---|---|
|  |  |  |
|  |  |  |
|  |  |  |
|  |  |  |
|  |  |  |
|  |  |  |

What patterns do you see? _____
_____
_____

Control of Chaos

# The Frenzy with My Work or Volunteering

It is important to identify when you find yourself becoming frenzied
at work or when you volunteer.
List the situation, who was there, what you did and what you wish you had done.

| Situation | Who was There | What I Did and What I Wish I had Done |
|---|---|---|
|  |  |  |
|  |  |  |
|  |  |  |
|  |  |  |
|  |  |  |

What patterns do you see? _____
_____
_____

# What Chaos Looks Like to Me

Chaos looks different to everyone.
Draw, doodle, sketch or write about what CHAOS looks like to you.

Control of Chaos

# Chaos Metaphors

A metaphor is a statement that compares two objects that are otherwise unrelated. It does not use *like* or *as*. (A simile uses *like* or *as*).

Example metaphors:
"Chaos *is a* whirlwind *that grabs me and tosses me away from what I want to focus on.*"
"*I am a bird caught in a thicket.*"

## Write some metaphors for *Frenzy* in your life

1) _____

2) _____

3) _____

4) _____

5) _____

## Write some metaphors for *Calm* in your life

1) _____

2) _____

3) _____

4) _____

5) _____

# Steps to Conquer Chaos

There are several primary steps you can take to conquer the chaos in your life.
For each of the steps below,
identify and list the ways you can achieve focus and control in your life.

Feel like you are in control

_____

_____

_____

_____

Begin ordering items

_____

_____

_____

_____

Limit distractions

_____

_____

_____

_____

Move on!

_____

_____

_____

_____

_____

Control of Chaos

# Bringing Order to Your Life

Although stress is a natural part of everyone's life, the feeling of
being unable to cope with chaos can affect your overall well-being.
Chaos is the mainstay of many people's lives.

In order to begin overcoming chaos in your life,
it will be helpful to examine where you are experiencing the majority of your chaos.
Identify what and who causes chaos and what and who
promotes calm in areas of your life.

| Area of My Life | What and Who Causes Chaos | What and Who Promotes Calmness |
|---|---|---|
| My Family | | |
| My Friends | | |
| At work or volunteering | | |
| In the Community | | |
| My Spirituality and/or Religion | | |
| Other | | |

What patterns do you see? _____

_____

_____

# Feng Shui

Feng Shui is the ancient Chinese practice of arranging your living or work space so that energy flows smoothly and you achieve harmony with your environment.

Below, rearrange your space so that there is less clutter and greater harmony.

Control of Chaos

# Type-A Personality

Often times, people with a Type-A Personality cause their own chaos.

The following quiz will help you explore whether or not you have a Type-A Personality. Answer the following questions by circling your responses.

| | | |
|---|---|---|
| I multi-task most of my day. | Yes | No |
| I have too many deadlines in my life | Yes | No |
| I dislike waiting in lines. | Yes | No |
| I get impatient easily | Yes | No |
| I eat very quickly. | Yes | No |
| I enjoy doing more than one thing at a time | Yes | No |
| I often can't sleep because my mind is racing | Yes | No |
| I have a chronic sense of time pressure. | Yes | No |
| I measure success by my accomplishments | Yes | No |
| I have a deep-seated need to be on time. | Yes | No |

SCORE = _____

---

For the above quiz, add the number of Yes answers you circled and put that number on the line for your score.

    If your score is from 0-3, you do not have a Type-A Personality.

    If your score is from 4-6, you have some Type-A Personality traits.

    If your score is from 7-10, you have a Type-A Personality.

How do you cause your own chaos in life by showing Type-A Personality traits?

_____

_____

_____

# Find a Place for Everything and Put Everything in Its Place

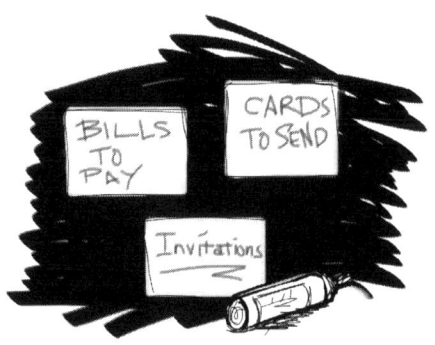

It is important to find places that you can easily get to when you need them. Below, list some of the items that you can better organize and put away.

| Items that Need a Place | Where You Can Put Items to Find them Easily |
|---|---|
|  |  |
|  |  |
|  |  |
|  |  |
|  |  |
|  |  |
|  |  |
|  |  |
|  |  |
|  |  |

Control of Chaos

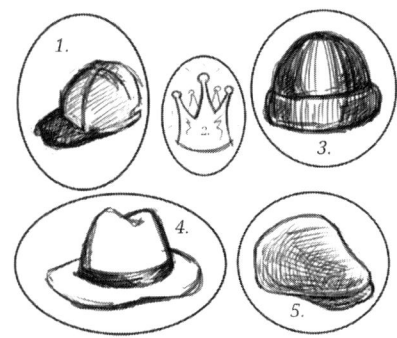

# Wearing Many Hats

The chaos in your life probably comes from wearing many hats and having many responsibilities.

Identify each hat and list all of the responsibilities you have with each hat you wear:

Hat 1 _____

_____
_____
_____
_____

Hat 2 _____

_____
_____
_____
_____

Hat 3 _____

_____
_____
_____
_____

Hat 4 _____

_____
_____
_____
_____

Hat 5 _____

_____
_____
_____
_____

## Superhero Syndrome

In today's fast-paced, chaotic lifestyle, many people get caught up in trying to be all things to all people.

The Superhero Syndrome emerges when people strive to accomplish everything in a perfect manner while meeting everyone else's needs.

In what ways do you try to be a superhero?

___

In which situations and with whom do you need to feel perfect with what you are doing?

___

Why do you feel the need to "do-it-all"?

___

Why do you want to be everything to everyone?

___

How can you lighten your load?

___

Control of Chaos

# Overcoming Technology Distractions

Distractions can cause you to feel chaotic — and — they can be eliminated.

Following are some ways in which you can complete your work without the distractions of electronic technology.

**Eliminate the need to continually check your e-mails.**

How can this help you accomplish more?

_____
_____

**Get away from the Internet.**

How can this help you accomplish more?

_____
_____

**Clear the clutter on your computer.**

How can this help you accomplish more?

_____
_____

**Watch less television.**

How can this help you accomplish more?

_____
_____

**Limit your time on social media sites.**

How can this help you accomplish more?

_____
_____

# My Chaos Letter

Write a letter to the chaos in your life.
This letter can address how you feel when you are in the midst of chaos,
why you find it difficult to avoid chaos and how it affects your life.

Dear Chaos,

_____
_____
_____
_____
_____
_____
_____
_____
_____
_____
_____
_____
_____
_____
_____
_____

*I want to get rid of you and I accept my responsibility in the matter. I am ready to move beyond a chaotic life.*

_____
Signature

Control of Chaos

# Stillness Inside You

> *In the midst of movement and chaos, keep stillness inside of you.*
> ~Deepak Chopra

What is Deepak Chopra saying in this quotation? _____
_____
_____
_____

When do you find yourself in the midst of chaos? _____
_____
_____
_____

With whom do you find yourself in the midst of chaos? _____
_____
_____
_____

How does this quote relate to your life? _____
_____
_____
_____

How can you best keep stillness inside you? _____
_____
_____
_____

# Juggling Multiple Roles

## Table of Contents and Facilitator Notes

Juggling Multiple Roles Introduction and Directions . . . . . . . 53
Juggling Multiple Roles Scale . . . . . . . . . . . . . . . . . . . . . . . . 54
Scoring Directions . . . . . . . . . . . . . . . . . . . . . . . . . . . . . . . . 55
Profile Interpretation . . . . . . . . . . . . . . . . . . . . . . . . . . . . . . 55
Expectations of Others . . . . . . . . . . . . . . . . . . . . . . . . . . . . 56

Example:

| ✓ | My Roles | This Person's Expectations |
|---|---|---|
| ✓ | Partner/Spouse | My wife thinks I should share all of the household duties equally but I work 50 hours a week and she works from home. I need to shop after work, help cook, etc. |

Expectations of Myself . . . . . . . . . . . . . . . . . . . . . . . . . . . . 57

Example:

| ✓ | My Roles | My Expectations of what I Do for and with This Person |
|---|---|---|
| ✓ | Employee/Employer | I am very grateful to my boss for giving me a job during hard times. Anything she asks of me, even if it's unreasonable, I am willing to do, no matter what. |

Time Spent in My Roles . . . . . . . . . . . . . . . . . . . . . . . . . . . 58

Example:

| ✓ | My Roles | Number of hours a day and how many days a week |
|---|---|---|
| ✓ | Grandparent/Grandchild | I babysit for my granddaughter 3 times a week for 10 hours each day while my daughter works. I cook for them also. I have other obligations, and don't have time for myself. |

Changes in My Roles. . . . . . . . . . . . . . . . . . . . . . . . . . . . . . 59

Example:

| Roles I Have Lost | Why I Lost the Role | If and How I Have Replaced the Role |
|---|---|---|
| I was the chairperson of my book club. | It was a 2-year term. | I accepted two other volunteer positions at my house of worship. |

Set Boundaries . . . . . . . . . . . . . . . . . . . . . . . . . . . . . . . . . . 60

*Read the definition of boundaries from the top of the handout. Ask for volunteers to tell what boundaries or limits they have set with others. Then, distribute the handout.*

Put Myself First . . . . . . . . . . . . . . . . . . . . . . . . . . . . . . . . . . 61

*After handout is completed, ask for a show of hands of each item as to how the group manages the nurturing activities. If anyone would like to share the benefit of engaging in that activity, encourage it.*

# Juggling Multiple Roles

## Table of Contents and Facilitator Notes

### Taking on New Roles ................................................. 62
*After participants have completed the handouts, divide them into pairs and ask them to read the completed handout to their partners, and vice versa. Allow them a few minutes to talk about their responses afterwards to the group, if they wish.*

### Shedding Unwanted Roles ........................................... 63
*Prior to distributing the handout, present this concept: Before accepting a new role, (committee member, care for someone, etc.) shed a role one is already participating in. Ask for comments about this idea.*

### What Are My Values? ................................................ 64
*If participants are having trouble thinking of values, suggest a few to get them started, i.e., honesty, integrity, approval, beauty, availability, etc.*

### Prioritizing My Roles ................................................ 65
*After participants have completed the handout, ask for a volunteer to write responses on the board and ask group members to call out their number one priority. Note similarities.*

### Delegating ........................................................... 66
*Discuss the value of delegating. Ask for two volunteers to role play. Tell them to delegate a task to the other. Ask one to do it in a demanding way and then the other to do it in a polite, assertive way.*

### Choices, Choices, Choices .......................................... 67
Example:

| My Roles | POOR Choices I Have Made | GOOD Choices I Have Made |
|---|---|---|
| Brother/Sister | I promised my brother that I would play cards with him twice a week even though my wife resented it. | I now have coordinated with my wife's schedule and play cards once a week with my brother. |

### Consequences of Role Overload .................................... 68
*After completing the handouts, ask for a volunteer to write results on the board. One by one, ask how many people checked off each item. Note the items that most people checked and discuss with the group.*

### My Ideal Role Script ................................................ 69
*After participants have written their scripts, ask if anyone would be willing to read a script aloud.*

### Chaos to the World Brings Uneasiness, but ...................... 70
*Suggest to participants that they might want to cut out the quotations and post them somewhere noticeable, as a reminder that chaos does allow for opportunities of creativity and growth.*

# Juggling Multiple Roles Scale Introduction and Directions

Juggling multiple roles and responsibilities requires you to wear many hats and find balance among the roles you play. This scale will assess your ability to juggle multiple life roles. Read each statement carefully. Circle the number of the response that shows how descriptive each statement is of you. Please answer all the questions to the best of your ability using the following scale.

In the following example, the circled 2 indicates that the statement is Somewhat True of the person completing the scale.

|  | True | Somewhat True | Not True |
|---|---|---|---|
| **I often find that…** | | | |
| I feel the need to do it all | 1 | ②  | 3 |

This is not a test and there are no right or wrong answers. Do not spend too much time thinking about your answers. Your initial response will be the most true for you. Be sure to respond to every statement.

*Turn to the next page and begin.*

Juggling Multiple Roles

Name _____ Date _____

# Juggling Multiple Roles Scale

|  | True | Somewhat True | Not True |
|---|---|---|---|

**I often find that...**

| | | | |
|---|---|---|---|
| I feel the need to do it all | 1 | 2 | 3 |
| I allow myself time to relax during the day | 3 | 2 | 1 |
| I find myself trying to please everyone | 1 | 2 | 3 |
| I find quiet time for myself | 3 | 2 | 1 |
| I feel that I have to be everything to everybody | 1 | 2 | 3 |
| I am assertive when I need to be | 3 | 2 | 1 |
| I can easily monitor and correct my negative self-talk | 3 | 2 | 1 |
| I constantly feel overwhelmed | 1 | 2 | 3 |
| I am adequately juggling family, career and social activities | 3 | 2 | 1 |
| I feel like I'm competing against myself | 1 | 2 | 3 |
| I try to excel in all of the roles I play | 1 | 2 | 3 |
| I cannot perform perfectly all the roles I play | 3 | 2 | 1 |
| I am comfortable saying no when I need to | 3 | 2 | 1 |
| I try to live up to the expectations of others | 1 | 2 | 3 |
| I have a support system to help me when I feel overwhelmed | 3 | 2 | 1 |
| I tend to take on more and more responsibility | 1 | 2 | 3 |
| I am constantly on the go | 1 | 2 | 3 |
| I do not concern myself about how others feel about me | 3 | 2 | 1 |
| I feel like I need to be perfect in all I do | 1 | 2 | 3 |
| I cope with stress well | 3 | 2 | 1 |
| I am having health problems from trying to do too much | 1 | 2 | 3 |
| I want to be everything to everyone | 1 | 2 | 3 |
| I try not to set impossible goals for myself | 3 | 2 | 1 |
| I am often too much of a perfectionist | 1 | 2 | 3 |
| I feel like I am fulfilling all of my obligations | 3 | 2 | 1 |

TOTAL = _____

*Go to the Scoring Directions on the next page*

# Juggling Multiple Roles Scale
# Scoring Directions

Part of living a chaotic life is not being able to juggle the multiple roles in our everyday lives. Add the numbers you circled on the scale and write that score on the line marked TOTAL. Then transfer that total to the space below:

**Juggling Multiple Roles Total = _____**

# Profile Interpretation

| Scales Scores | Result | Indications |
|---|---|---|
| Scores from 59 to 75 | High | If you score in the high range, you seem to be juggling your multiple life roles well. |
| Scores from 42 to 58 | Moderate | If you score in the moderate range, you seem to be fairly successful in juggling your multiple life roles. |
| Scores from 25 to 41 | Low | If you score in the low range, you seem to be having difficulty juggling your multiple life roles. |

No matter how you scored, low, moderate or high, you will benefit from these exercises. By going to the next section and completing the activities that follow, you will greatly enhance your chances of being successful at juggling multiple life roles.

Juggling Multiple Roles

# Expectations of Others

Your time may be claimed in many different ways from a variety of people.

It is important to identify the many roles you play and what is expected of you. Complete the following table below and on another blank page if needed.

| ✔ | My Roles | This Person's Expectations |
|---|---|---|
|   | Partner / Spouse |   |
|   | Son / Daughter |   |
|   | Brother / Sister |   |
|   | Parent |   |
|   | Grandparent / Grandchild |   |
|   | Other Relative |   |
|   | Friend |   |
|   | Neighbor |   |
|   | Employee / Employer |   |
|   | Student |   |
|   | Volunteer |   |
|   | Hobbyist |   |
|   | Other |   |
|   | Other |   |

Which roles that you checked above take the most commitment from you?

_____

_____

Which roles that you checked above take the least commitment from you?

_____

_____

Juggling Multiple Roles

# Expectations of Myself

Often, people who are in our life do not expect as much from us as we do from ourselves.
It is important to identify whether your expectations of yourself
are realistic or unrealistic.
Complete the following table below and on another blank page if needed.

| ✔ | My Roles | My Expectations of what I Do for and with this Person |
|---|---|---|
|   | Partner / Spouse |   |
|   | Son / Daughter |   |
|   | Brother / Sister |   |
|   | Parent |   |
|   | Grandparent / Grandchild |   |
|   | Other Relative |   |
|   | Friend |   |
|   | Neighbor |   |
|   | Employee / Employer |   |
|   | Student |   |
|   | Volunteer |   |
|   | Hobbyist |   |
|   | Other |   |
|   | Other |   |

Which roles that you checked above are realistic?

_____

_____

Which roles that you checked above are unrealistic?

_____

_____

Juggling Multiple Roles

# Time Spent in My Roles

You commit various amounts of time to the roles you play.
Place a check mark in front of the roles you play and
indicate the amount of time you spend each day engaged in that role.

| ✔ | My Roles | Number of Hours a Day and How Many Days a Week |
|---|---|---|
| | Partner / Spouse | |
| | Son / Daughter | |
| | Brother / Sister | |
| | Parent | |
| | Grandparent / Grandchild | |
| | Other Relative | |
| | Friend | |
| | Neighbor | |
| | Employee / Employer | |
| | Student | |
| | Volunteer | |
| | Hobbyist | |
| | Other | |
| | Other | |

What roles take the most amount of time?
_____
_____

What roles take the least amount of time?
_____
_____

Juggling Multiple Roles

# Changes in My Roles

How have the roles you have played changed in the past year?
Oftentimes, you add or lose roles that can add to the chaos in your life.
Note how your roles have changed and the impact these changes have had on your life.
Identify the roles you have lost, why you lost them, and if you have replaced the roles.

| Roles I Have Lost | Why I Lost the Role | If and How I Have Replaced the Role |
|---|---|---|
| | | |
| | | |
| | | |
| | | |
| | | |
| | | |

Identify the roles you have gained, why you gained them, and how they are affecting you.

| Roles I Have Gained | Why I Gained the Role | How This Role Is Affecting My Life |
|---|---|---|
| | | |
| | | |
| | | |
| | | |
| | | |
| | | |

Juggling Multiple Roles

# Set Boundaries

To avoid overload in any or all of your roles, you need to set boundaries.
Boundaries are guidelines, rules and limits that you identify as
safe and permissible ways for others to behave around you.
An example of a boundary might be in speaking to a neighbor:
*"Please don't come over if all you are going to do is gossip about others in the neighborhood.
If you agree not to gossip, then I would love to have you come over!"*
Write about the various roles you play and the boundaries you need to set.

| ✔ | My Roles | Boundaries I Need to Set |
|---|---|---|
| | Partner / Spouse | |
| | Son / Daughter | |
| | Brother / Sister | |
| | Parent | |
| | Grandparent / Grandchild | |
| | Other Relative | |
| | Friend | |
| | Neighbor | |
| | Employee / Employer | |
| | Student | |
| | Volunteer | |
| | Hobbyist | |
| | Other | |
| | Other | |

# Put Myself First

By putting yourself first, you can reduce anxiety of juggling multiple roles through small acts of kindness toward yourself. Allow yourself to make time each day to nurture yourself, away from your duties at work and home.

Some of the nurturing activities you can do for yourself are listed below. Place a check in the box in front of those you already do and a check after the item you plan to do.

❏ Take a walk ❏
❏ Take a long bubble bath ❏
❏ Go to a matinee movie ❏
❏ Meditate ❏
❏ Watch a sunset ❏
❏ Watch children play ❏
❏ Plant a garden ❏
❏ Listen to your favorite music ❏
❏ Play with a pet ❏
❏ Do yoga ❏
❏ Read a book ❏
❏ Drink a cup of tea ❏
❏ Take a class ❏
❏ _____ ❏
❏ _____ ❏
❏ _____ ❏
❏ _____ ❏
❏ _____ ❏

❏ Get a massage ❏
❏ Read an inspirational book ❏
❏ Work on a crossword puzzle ❏
❏ Write in a journal ❏
❏ Go to a local park ❏
❏ Visit friends ❏
❏ Rent and watch videos ❏
❏ Browse in a bookstore ❏
❏ Ride a horse ❏
❏ Visit a museum ❏
❏ Learn a foreign language ❏
❏ Play computer games ❏
❏ Play sports ❏
❏ _____ ❏
❏ _____ ❏
❏ _____ ❏
❏ _____ ❏
❏ _____ ❏

Juggling Multiple Roles

# Taking on New Roles

You may want to take on some new roles in your life.
If so, following are some of the questions you need to ask yourself
in taking on a new role.

New role I'm thinking about adding: _____
_____
_____
_____

How does the role fit with my value system? Why? _____
_____
_____
_____
_____

How will this new role benefit me or not? Why? _____
_____
_____
_____
_____

What will I need to sacrifice? _____
_____
_____
_____
_____

What goal will it help me achieve? _____
_____
_____
_____
_____

How will this enhance my life satisfaction?_____
_____
_____
_____
_____

Juggling Multiple Roles

# Shedding Unwanted Roles

You may want to eliminate some of the roles in your life, especially if you have assumed a new role.

Following are some of the questions you need to ask yourself in shedding an existing role.

Present role I'm thinking about shedding: _____
_____
_____
_____

How does the role not fit with my value system? _____
_____
_____
_____

Will shedding this role benefit me or not? Why? _____
_____
_____
_____

What will I be sacrificing? _____
_____
_____
_____

What goal will this help me achieve? _____
_____
_____
_____

How will shedding this role enhance my life satisfaction? _____
_____
_____
_____

# What Are My Values?

When the roles you play do not correspond with your
basic value system, you may experience chaos.
In the spaces below, draw or write about your four most basic values.

# Prioritizing My Roles

Rank your roles in the order of importance to you.

| Rank # | Roles | Why Did I Rank It This Way? |
|---|---|---|
| 1 | | |
| 2 | | |
| 3 | | |
| 4 | | |
| 5 | | |
| 6 | | |
| 7 | | |
| 8 | | |
| 9 | | |
| 10 | | |

Juggling Multiple Roles

# Delegating

Delegating is assigning responsibility for a task to another person.
Delegating will free up time for you to do other things or just enjoy yourself.
Look for ways to ask others to help you so that you do not feel overloaded.

| What I Want to Delegate | To Whom I Want to Delegate | How This Will help Me |
|---|---|---|
|  |  |  |
|  |  |  |
|  |  |  |
|  |  |  |
|  |  |  |
|  |  |  |
|  |  |  |
|  |  |  |

When you delegate, are you bossy? _____

Tactful? _____

Assertive but not demanding? _____

How can you delegate successfully? _____

_____

_____

Juggling Multiple Roles

# Choices, Choices, Choices

Feelings of frustration in the roles you play
are often the result of good and poor choices you have made.
Identify the poor choices and good choices you have made
in the various roles you play.

| My Roles | POOR Choices I Have Made | GOOD Choices I Have Made |
|---|---|---|
| Partner / Spouse | | |
| Son / Daughter | | |
| Brother / Sister | | |
| Parent | | |
| Grandparent / Grandchild | | |
| Other Relative | | |
| Friend | | |
| Neighbor | | |
| Employee / Employer | | |
| Student | | |
| Volunteer | | |
| Hobbyist | | |
| Other | | |
| Other | | |

# Juggling Multiple Roles

# Consequences of Role Overload

Juggling multiple roles can be both frustrating and stress-filled.
When your demands exceed your resources for managing them, stress is the result.
Look at the consequences of role overload below.
Check the ones that apply to you, and then describe their effects on you.

❑ Strain in my relationships _____

❑ Strain in family harmony _____

❑ Problems with my physical health _____

❑ Problems with my mental health _____

❑ Hostility _____

❑ Lack of sleep _____

❑ Overeating _____

❑ Poor appetite _____

❑ Anxiousness _____

❑ Panic attacks _____

❑ Sadness _____

❑ Depression _____

❑ Unhealthy substances _____

❑ Increase in cigarette smoking _____

❑ Flair-ups in my community _____

❑ Increased risk-taking behaviors _____

❑ Other _____

❑ Other _____

❑ Other _____

# My Ideal Role Script

Write a scenario and create a new role you want to play,
a role that you feel would be *ideal*.

Juggling Multiple Roles

# Chaos to the World Brings Uneasiness, but …

> *Chaos to the world brings uneasiness,*
> *but it also allows the opportunity for creativity and growth.*
> ~ Thomas Barrett

How does chaos make you feel uneasy? _____
_____
_____
_____

How can chaos bring an opportunity for creativity? _____
_____
_____
_____

How can chaos bring an opportunity for growth? _____
_____
_____
_____

How can you use chaos to enhance your life? _____
_____
_____
_____

What does this quote mean to you? _____
_____
_____
_____

# Time-Pressure

## Table of Contents and Facilitator Notes

**Time-Pressure Introduction and Directions** . . . . . . . . . . . . . . .73
**Time-Pressure Scale**. . . . . . . . . . . . . . . . . . . . . . . . . . . . . .74–75
**Scoring Directions** . . . . . . . . . . . . . . . . . . . . . . . . . . . . . . . . . .76
**Profile Interpretation** . . . . . . . . . . . . . . . . . . . . . . . . . . . . . . .76
**Negative Time-Pressure Behaviors** . . . . . . . . . . . . . . . . . . . . .77

*After completing the handout, ask for volunteers to tell the group how they feel when they are pressured for time.*

**Feelings When Facing Too Much Time-Pressure**. . . . . . . . . . .78

*After completing the handout, discuss with the group if they have the same feelings as those in the word search, and ask if they have any others.*

**What I Procrastinate About**. . . . . . . . . . . . . . . . . . . . . . . . . . .79

*Prior to distributing handouts, ask the participants the meaning of procrastinating (putting off tasks for another time). Ask for a show of hands: "How many of you procrastinate?"*

**Time Caricatures** . . . . . . . . . . . . . . . . . . . . . . . . . . . . . . . . . . .80

*After completing the handout, ask for volunteers to show their caricature to the group and talk about it.*

**Reasons I Procrastinate**. . . . . . . . . . . . . . . . . . . . . . . . . . . . . .81

*After completing the handout, ask for a show of hands for a count of who colored in the various circles. Note which were the most common reasons.*

**My Time Clock** . . . . . . . . . . . . . . . . . . . . . . . . . . . . . . . . . . . . .82

*After the participants finish the handout, ask for a show of hands: "Who are morning people?" "Who are evening people?" "Who are both?" "Who are neither?" Ask for a show of hands if the people they live with are the same as they are.*

**Time Slips Away at Home** . . . . . . . . . . . . . . . . . . . . . . . . . . . .83

Example:

| How Time Can Slip Away | When This Happens | Why This Happens |
|---|---|---|
| Socializing | When I am on the computer | I just focus and don't pay attention to anything around me. |

Time-Pressure

# Table of Contents and Facilitator Notes

## Time Slips Away at Work or Other Places...........84
Example:

| How Time Can Slip Away | When This Happens | Why This Happens |
|---|---|---|
| *Misplacing Things* | *All day long* | *I have so many different things to do I don't have time to file or find place for everything.* |

## Time Fears ...........85
*After participants have completed the worksheet, ask for volunteers who might want to share their insights into what they realized about themselves.*

## Slow Down!...........86
*Prior to distributing the handouts, ask how many people feel they rush through life.*

## I Feel Driven! ...........87
*After participants have completed the handouts, ask for a volunteer to write on the board and ask people to tell ways people go fast. Notice the most common responses.*

## Multitasking ...........88

| What I Do | How it Affects the Quality of What I am Doing | How it Affects My Stress-Level |
|---|---|---|
| *Just come home from work, feed the baby, make dinner, set the table, wash lunch dishes and talk on the phone to my committee people, all at the same time.* | *I probably don't pay as much attention to the other children as I would like. Not sure I do the best on anything I am doing.* | *I get aggravated with everyone even though it's no one's fault. I shout at the other children to get ready for dinner and get angry at my husband who just walked in, for not helping.* |

## My Involuntary Obligations ...........89
*Prior to distributing handouts, ask participants what types of obligations they have that they didn't ask for or want.*

## Changing My Involuntary Obligations...........90
Example:

| My Involuntary Obligations | How I Can Discontinue | How Life Would be Calmer |
|---|---|---|
| *I have been going to my elderly aunt's house everyday on the way home from work to check on her.* | *I can ask other relatives, the neighbors and call social services to arrange for someone to come to the house.* | *I could go once a week on the weekend and then come straight home from work without needing to rush to get dinner finished.* |

# Time-Pressure Scale
# Introduction and Directions

Time is a universal feature of life. Feeling pressured to get everything finished in a certain amount of time can lead to chaos in everyday life in the form of feeling rushed, harried, hassled, frustrated and anxious. In return, this chaos can lead to greater problems including a higher level of hostility, emotional and physical pain, and a lower quality of life.

The Time-Pressure Scale can help you identify and explore the impact that poor time management skills is having on your overall level of life chaos.

This assessment contains 28 statements related to your time management habits. Read each of the statements and decide whether or not the statement describes you. If the statement does describe you, circle the number in the YES column. If the statement does not describe you, circle the number in the NO column.

In the following example, the circled number under YES indicates the statement is descriptive of the person completing the inventory.

|  | YES | NO |
|---|---|---|
| I feel a constant sense of time-pressure | (2) | 1 |

This is not a test and there are no right or wrong answers. Do not spend too much time thinking about your answers. Your initial response will be the most true for you. Be sure to respond to every statement.

*Turn to the next page and begin.*

# Time-Pressure Scale

|  | YES | NO |
|---|---|---|
| I feel a constant sense of time-pressure | 2 | 1 |
| I never take time for leisure activities | 2 | 1 |
| I measure myself by my accomplishments | 2 | 1 |
| My mind seems to be constantly racing | 2 | 1 |
| I feel driven | 2 | 1 |
| I do most things quickly | 2 | 1 |
| I have high expectations of myself | 2 | 1 |

**A - TOTAL** _____

| | | |
|---|---|---|
| I am being pulled in too many directions | 2 | 1 |
| I do things just to avoid disappointing others | 2 | 1 |
| I say yes to tasks to which I really should say no | 2 | 1 |
| I let people walk all over me | 2 | 1 |
| I have trouble setting and sticking to boundaries | 2 | 1 |
| I always say yes when people ask me to do something they need | 2 | 1 |
| I take on way more tasks than I can complete | 2 | 1 |

**O - TOTAL** _____

*Continued on the next page*

## Time-Pressure Scale *Continued*

|  | YES | NO |
|---|---|---|
| I must be perfect in all I do and I avoid what I can't do perfectly | 2 | 1 |
| I have a difficult time getting started to complete tasks | 2 | 1 |
| I become distracted easily and often cannot finish tasks | 2 | 1 |
| I have a difficult time prioritizing my tasks | 2 | 1 |
| I often postpone tasks I don't like to do | 2 | 1 |
| When I complete tasks, I need them to be perfect | 2 | 1 |
| I have to do projects the right way or I don't want to do them at all | 2 | 1 |

P - TOTAL _____

| | YES | NO |
|---|---|---|
| I constantly feel pressured about my schedule | 2 | 1 |
| I always have tight deadlines | 2 | 1 |
| I tend to rush even though rushing is not necessary | 2 | 1 |
| I always seem to be doing many tasks at one time | 2 | 1 |
| I don't take time to enjoy the tasks I complete | 2 | 1 |
| I am always worried about something I need to do in the future | 2 | 1 |
| I don't take time to slow down | 2 | 1 |

R - TOTAL _____

*Go to the Scoring Directions on the next page*

Time-Pressure

# Time-Pressure Scale Scoring Directions

The Time-Pressure Scale is designed to help you identify the ways that you mismanage your time and cause additional chaos in your life. On the previous two pages, add the numbers that you circled in each section and write the scores on each of the TOTAL lines. You will receive a total in the range from 7 to 14. Next transfer those numbers to the spaces below. Afterwards, total all four scale totals to give you your grand total.

| | | | | |
|---|---|---|---|---|
| A | Type-A Personality | Total | = | _____ |
| O | Unwanted Obligations | Total | = | _____ |
| P | Procrastination | Total | = | _____ |
| R | Rushing | Total | = | _____ |

GRAND TOTAL = _____

# Profile Interpretation

| Individual Scale Score | Grand Total Scale Score | Result | Indications |
|---|---|---|---|
| 7 to 9 | 28 to 37 | Low | You do feel much time pressure. You seem to have good time-management skills. |
| 10 to 11 | 38 to 46 | Moderate | You have some time-pressure. You would benefit from practicing some new time-management skills. |
| 12 to 14 | 47 to 56 | High | You have a great deal of time-pressure. You need to work on your time-management skills. |

No matter how you scored on the Time-Pressure Scale (Low, Moderate or High), you will benefit from doing all of the following exercises.

Time-Pressure

# Negative Time-Pressure Behaviors

Check the ways you tend to behave when you are feeling pressure regarding your time and write about how you feel at that time and how it affects you.

I worry excessively about keeping to a schedule. _____
_____
_____

I try to be perfect in all of my activities and projects. _____
_____
_____

I make and try to keep very tight deadlines at home. _____
_____
_____

I make and try to keep very tight deadlines at work. _____
_____
_____

I rush when rushing is not necessary. _____
_____
_____

I do several things at one time. _____
_____
_____

I feel the need to always be early. _____
_____
_____

I do not take time to enjoy my life. _____
_____
_____

Can you promise yourself to remember NOT to behave in the way(s) you just wrote about above? What can you do? _____
_____
_____

Time-Pressure

# Feelings When Facing Too Much Time-Pressure Word Search

Circle the fourteen words that represent feelings of time-pressure.
Words appear across, backwards, up, down, and diagonal.
See the words below.

```
D E M L E H W R E V O Z V A
S E P R E S S U R E R U M F
H K L R D N P E R I O R O R
A L P M E F R E N Z I E D U
R A N X I O U S T C O W N S
R Z A E R L S O H M Q E N T
I P R X R G S P Q A Z E M R
E P O A A U D D A O V G W A
D P R O H U R R Y I N G G T
R U S H E D E E R P N E S E
E M X E X T R D D L I E J D
C H A O T I C O P E F J D D
D E L S S A H H O S T I L E
```

Look for the following words:
- ANXIOUS
- CHAOTIC
- DEADLINES
- DRIVEN
- FRENZY
- FRUSTRATED
- HARRIED
- HASSLED
- HOSTILE
- HURRY
- OVERWHELMED
- PAINED
- PRESSURE
- RUSHED

# What I Procrastinate About

People procrastinate about all different kinds of things.

List what you tend to put off when you are *at home*, why and how it affects you.

| What I Put Off | Why I Put It Off | What Is the Effect? |
|---|---|---|
|  |  |  |
|  |  |  |
|  |  |  |
|  |  |  |
|  |  |  |

List what you tend to put off when you are *at work, volunteering, or in a club, organization, group or community* and how it affects you.

| What I Put Off | Why I Put It Off | What Is the Effect? |
|---|---|---|
|  |  |  |
|  |  |  |
|  |  |  |
|  |  |  |
|  |  |  |

Time-Pressure

# Time Caricatures

Caricatures are exaggerated or distorted likenesses.
You don't need to be an artist to draw caricatures, the drawing just needs to make sense to you to show what you feel like when you are experiencing time-pressure.

Draw a caricature that represents your time-pressure.

# Reasons I Procrastinate

People procrastinate for a wide variety of reasons.
Think about the reasons that you procrastinate in life.
Put an X over the circles that do not apply to you.
Then, color in the circle that represents the reason that you procrastinate the most.
Next to it, write why.

Now that you have identified your reasons for procrastinating, what can you do better?

_____
_____
_____

Time-Pressure

# My Time Clock

Most people are either morning people or evening people. The following quiz will help you determine which type you are and when you are probably most productive in getting tasks accomplished.

**A.**

| | | |
|---|---|---|
| I like to sleep in and would do so every day.. | YES | NO |
| I rarely see the sun come up. | YES | NO |
| I love watching late-night television. | YES | NO |
| I am not disturbed when light comes in my room in the morning. | YES | NO |
| I do my best work in the evenings. | YES | NO |

A. TOTAL = _____

**B.**

| | | |
|---|---|---|
| An 8-5 job fits my personality | YES | NO |
| Even if I do not go to work, I wake up early in the morning | YES | NO |
| I go to bed early. | YES | NO |
| I tape light-night television shows to watch them during the day. | YES | NO |
| I feel refreshed in the morning. | YES | NO |

B. TOTAL = _____

Count the number of items you said "Yes" to in each section. If your total was higher for the **A Group, you are a late-night person**. If your total was higher for the **B Group, you are a morning person**. If it was even or off one or two, **you are both a morning person and an evening person**, or **neither**. How can you start using your time clock to help you be more productive each day?

_____

_____

_____

Time-Pressure

# Time Slips Away at Home

If you think about your habits related to time,
you will notice specific patterns of the ways time seems to slip away from you.
In the spaces that follow, list the ways that time slips away from you at home.

| How Time Can Slip Away | When This Happens | Why This Happens |
|---|---|---|
| Socializing | | |
| Misplacing things | | |
| Forgetting things | | |
| Becoming very involved in what I am doing | | |
| Surfing the Internet | | |
| Reading e-mails | | |
| Being late | | |
| Procrastinating | | |
| Other | | |

What patterns do you see?

_____

_____

_____

Time-Pressure

# Time Fears

People with time urgency have intense fears
that trigger their time problems.
Think about the following fears about time
and how they manifest themselves.
Complete the sentence starters, keeping TIME in mind.

By trying to please other people, I _____

_____

_____

By trying to meet everyone else's needs but my own, I _____

_____

_____

By waiting until the last moment, I _____

_____

_____

By taking on too many tasks, I _____

_____

_____

By always having to be perfect, I _____

_____

_____

By setting expectations that are too high for myself, I _____

_____

_____

# Time-Pressure

## Slow Down!
Slowing down to the normal speed of life can help you deal with your time-pressures.

Please describe a situation when you find yourself always rushing. _____
_____
_____
_____
_____

How can you worry less about the future and stay in the present moment? _____
_____
_____
_____
_____

How can you worry less about a deadline for the activity? _____
_____
_____
_____
_____

How can you worry less about doing the activity perfectly? _____
_____
_____
_____
_____

How can you think of the activity as not a competition or an accomplishment? _____
_____
_____
_____
_____

Time-Pressure

# I Feel Driven!

**Identify ten ways that you feel driven to go faster
(driving to get to work, speaking quickly, walking and eating faster, etc.)**

1. _____
   _____

2. _____
   _____

3. _____
   _____

4. _____
   _____

5. _____
   _____

6. _____
   _____

7. _____
   _____

8. _____
   _____

9. _____
   _____

10. _____
    _____

# Multitasking

People often believe that multitasking (doing two or more things at one time) is the best way to be more productive. In fact, multi-tasking often reduces productivity. List the two or three activities you do when multitasking, how it affects the quality of what you are doing and how it affects your stress-level.

| What I Do | How It Affects the Quality of What I Am Doing | How It Affects My Stress-Level |
|---|---|---|
|  |  |  |
|  |  |  |
|  |  |  |
|  |  |  |
|  |  |  |
|  |  |  |

If you find that certain activities are negatively affected by multitasking, how can you begin to focus on one activity at a time?

_____
_____
_____
_____

Time-Pressure

# My Involuntary Obligations

We all have obligations in our lives.
Some of these obligations we happily volunteered to do, while others are the result of having them given to us or our having no choice in the matter.

| My Involuntary Obligation | Who Gave It to Me? or Why Did I Feel I Had No Choice? | How Much of My Time and Energy Does This Take? |
|---|---|---|
|  |  |  |
|  |  |  |
|  |  |  |
|  |  |  |
|  |  |  |
|  |  |  |
|  |  |  |

What patterns emerge?

_____

_____

_____

Time-Pressure

# Changing My Involuntary Obligations

Involuntary obligations can take a great deal of your time each week
and create a perpetual state of chaos.
To make life calmer, it would help to discontinue
some of these obligations, if possible.

| My Involuntary Obligations | How I Can Discontinue | How Life Would be Calmer |
|---|---|---|
| | | |
| | | |
| | | |
| | | |
| | | |
| | | |
| | | |

What patterns emerge?

_____

_____

_____

Whole Person Associates is the leading publisher of training resources for professionals who empower people to create and maintain healthy lifestyles. Our creative resources will help you work effectively with your clients in the areas of stress management, wellness promotion, mental health and life skills.

Please visit us at our web site: **Wholeperson.com**. You can check out our entire line of products, place an order, request our print catalog, and sign up for our monthly special notifications.

**Whole Person Associates**

800-247-6789